WORSHIP TOGETHER

www.worshiptogether.com

SONGBOOK 2.0

Table of Contents

Agnus Dei

Words and Music by
MICHAEL W. SMITH

Lord, God_____ al - might - y. Wor-thy is the

Lamb, wor-thy is the Lamb. A -

1.
A2

2.
A2

men. men.

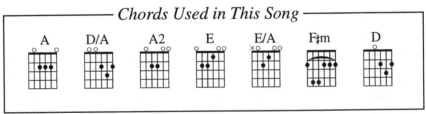

All I Know

Words and Music by
IAN WHITE

Moderately

1. Though I feel a-fraid__ of ter-ri-tory__ un-known, I
(2.) lies a-cross the waves__ may cause my heart__ to fear; Will

know that I__ can say that I do not stand__ a-lone. For
I sur-vive__ the day, must I leave what's known__ and dear? A

Je-sus, You have pro-mised Your pre-sence in__ my heart; I__
ship that's in the har-bour is still and safe__ from harm; but it

can-not see__ the end-ing, but it's here that I__ must start. And
was not built__ to be there, it was made for wind__ and storm.

All I'm Asking For

Words and Music by
**TOM LANE and
MIKE DEMUS**

Take my hand, lead me, Lord. Take me to Your door. Cov-er me with Your blood. That's all I'm ask-ing for. That's all I'm ask-ing for.

Ev-'ry
It's a

Be Glorified

Words and Music by
LOUIE GIGLIO
and CHRIS TOMLIN

Your love— has cap-tured— me,— Your grace— has set me— free;— Your life,— the air I— breathe.—

Be glo-ri-fied— in me.—

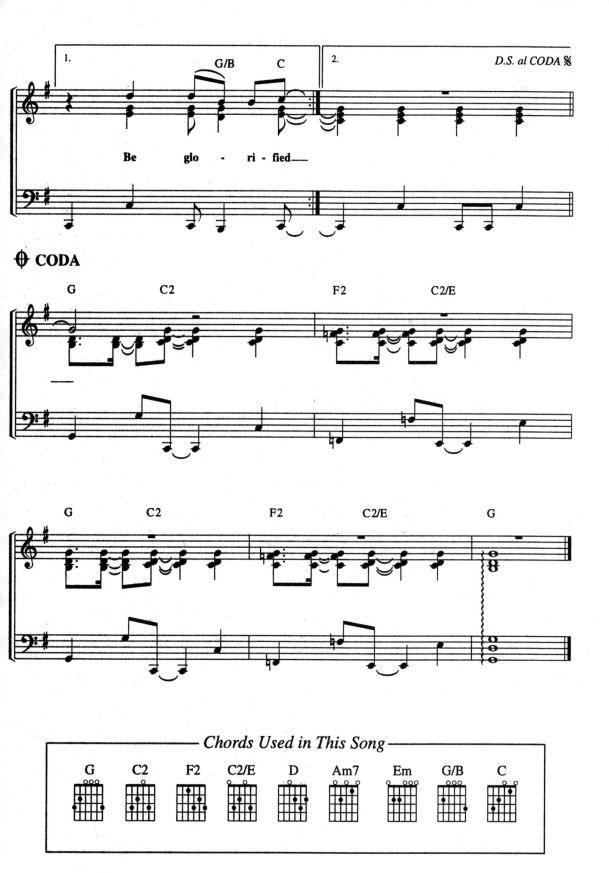

Be glo - ri - fied____

CODA

Chords Used in This Song

G C2 F2 C2/E D Am7 Em G/B C

Beautiful Savior
(All My Days)

Words and Music by STUART TOWNEND

vs. 3 I long to be where the praise is never ending;
Yearn to dwell where the glory never fades,
Where countless worshipers will share one song,
And cries of 'worthy' will honor the Lamb!

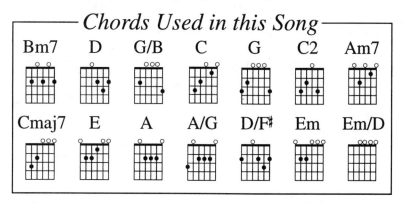

Chords Used in this Song

Bm7 D G/B C G C2 Am7

Cmaj7 E A A/G D/F♯ Em Em/D

6 Better Is One Day

Words and Music by
MATT REDMAN

With a strong beat

1. How love-ly is Your dwell-ing place,
(2.) thing I ask and I would seek:

O Lord al-might-y. For my soul longs and
to see Your beau-ty, to find You in the

e-ven faints for You. For
place Your glo-ry dwells. One

here my heart is sat-is-fied with-in Your pres-
thing I ask and I would seek: to see Your beau-

Calling Out Your Name

Words and Music by
GREG and REBECCA SPARKS

Calm Faith

Words and Music by
IAN WHITE

Prayerfully

1. A prayer from the in-ner heart____ we bring to
(2.) know that what____ we stand____ for stays the

You. For deep un-spo-ken
same. And 'til the end of

cries are break-ing through. For
time, Your love re-mains.

You love____ us like no oth-er can,____

2. (Bb) pas - sion for souls._____ We're ask - ing for

(F) calm (C) faith; we're ask - ing for burn - (Gm) ing

(F) love. We're ask - ing for bright (Gm) hope and a

(C) deep com - pas - sion for_____ (F) souls.

Chords Used in This Song

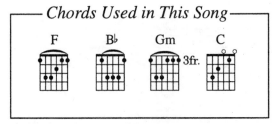

Encounter

Words and Music by
IAN WHITE

With praise

1. You bring us Your Word,⎯ we bring You a prayer,⎯ some-times so weak⎯ and close to de-spair.⎯ We sense all our wrong⎯ in the face of Your right.⎯ We pray to be strong⎯ to be filled with Your fire.⎯ 2. We long for Your life,⎯

For as Long as I Live
(Psalm 116)

**Words and Music by
IAN WHITE**

Capo 2 (D)

Chords Used in This Song

Em7　A7　D　F#m7　Bm7　G　A7sus　A

For the Cross

11

Words and Music by
MATT and BETH REDMAN

With a strong rhythm

1. I will love You for the____ cross,
2. You came in-to a world of____ shame,
3. Je-sus Christ, the sin-ner's____ friend;
4. O the mys-t'ry of the____ cross,

and I will love You for the____ cost:
and paid the price we could not____ pay:
does this kind-ness know no____ bounds?
You were pun-ished, You were____ crushed;

Man of suf-fer-ings,____ bring-er of my peace,
death that brought me life,____ blood that brought me home.
With Your pre-cious blood____ You have pur-chased me.____
but that pun-ish-ment____ has be-come my peace.____

Chords Used in This Song

Bm A G D F♯m7 Gmaj7

Free to Live

Words and Music by
IAN WHITE

With praise

stand on the shore of an o - cean, gaz - ing out to
stand look - ing out on a hill - side watch - ing the sun go

sea. He casts my sins to the wa - ters and
down. He caus - es me now to love Him

Chords Used in This Song

Freedom Song

Words and Music by
CHARLIE HALL

Chords Used in This Song

G C2 D Em Dsus Am7 D2/A

Glorify

Capo 2 (D)

**Words and Music by
LINDA BARNHILL**

1. Glo - ri - fy _____ Your name, _____
2. Je - sus, _____ light the flame. _____
3. Pu - ri - fy _____ Your bride, _____

glo - ri - fy _____ Your name.
Je - sus, _____ light the flame.
pu - ri - fy _____ Your bride.

Chords Used in This Song

D   C   G

Glory to You

Words and Music by
JENNIFER MARTIN

Hallelujah Song

Words and Music by
MATT REDMAN

16

17
Happiness Is You

Words and Music by
JOHN HARTLEY
and GARY SADLER

Joyfully

You fill my heart____ with_ a song____ to_ Your name.
You bring me joy,____ cause_ my mourn - ing____ to end.

You dry my tears,____ turn_ my fears
Beau - ti - ful ash - es,____ I'm danc -

to praise.____
-in'__ a - gain.____

And e - ven in__ my trou -
And gaz - ing on__ Your beau -

3rd time to CODA

- bles, You will see me through.
- ty, what trea - sure I have found.

Je - sus,____ hap - pi - ness__ is You.

Chords Used in This Song

18
Have You Heard the Good News?

Words and Music by
STUART GARRARD

Have you heard the good news?___ Have you heard the good news?___ We can live___ in hope___ ___ be-cause of what the Lord___ has done.___ Have you

1.3.5.

2.4.6. *Fine*

1. There is a way___ when there seems___
2. A hope for jus - tice ___ and___

19 Hear the Music of My Heart

Words and Music by
MATT REDMAN

Strong and rhythmic

1. Lord, hear the mus - ic of my heart;
2. You've be - come the rul - er of my heart;

hear all the pour - ings of my soul.
You've be - come the lov - er of my soul.

Songs tell - ing of a life of love:

Je - sus, this is all for You. You've be - come the Sav - ior of

Here I Am
(I Will Always Love Your Name)

20

Words and Music by
PAUL OAKLEY

With spirit ♩ = 116

1. Here I__ am,____ and I have__ come__ to
(2.) took my__ sin,____ You took my__ shame,__ You
(3.) bid me__ come,____ You make me__ whole,__ You

thank You,__ Lord,____ for all You've done;____
drank my__ cup,____ You bore my pain;____
give me__ peace,____ You re - store my soul;____

thank__ You, Lord.____
thank__ You, Lord.____
thank__ You, Lord.____

You paid the__ price____ at
You broke the__ curse,____ You
You fill me__ up,____ and

21

History Maker

With energy

Words and Music by
MARTIN SMITH

1. Is it true____ to-day
   (2.) ____ to-day
   (3.) ____ to-day
   (4.) - a - cles,

that, when peo-
that, when peo-
that, when peo-
we'll see an -

- ple pray,
- ple pray,
- ple stand
- gels sing,

cloud - less skies____
we'll see dead
with the fire
we'll see bro -

____ will break,
____ men rise
____ of God
- ken hearts

kings and queens
and the blind____
and the truth
mak - ing his -

____ will shake?
____ set free?
____ in hand,
- to - ry?

1.2.4. / to next section

Yes, it's true,____

3.

4. We'll see mir -

Chords Used in This Song

22

House of Gold

Words and Music by
PAUL OAKLEY

1. Your voice is like thun - der,
2. Your grace is so ten - der,

Your eyes like fi - re,
Your love like wine.

Your throne is for - ev - er,
To You I sur - ren - der;

in un - ap - proach - a - ble light.

2.

Cmaj7   D

I lay down my life.___   And all___ I want to do

G   D   C

is to build___ a house___ of gold,___
Be my wis - dom and be___ my strength,___

G   D   Em

pur - est sil - ver and cost - ly___ stones.___
fill me up with Your faith - ful - ness,___

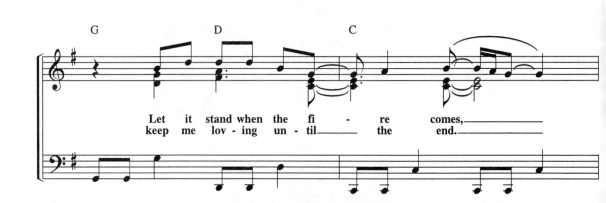

G   D   C

Let it stand when the fi - re comes,___
keep me lov - ing un - til___ the end.___

23 How I Love Your Name

Words and Music by
GARY SADLER and RICK CUA

Chords Used in This Song

I Am Yours

Capo 3 (D)

With life

Words and Music by
MATT REDMAN

1. God of res - to - ra - tion,
2. Sing-ing of a love now,

my hope is in the life You bring to me.
You taught this bro - ken heart to sing a - gain.

Heal - er of my wounds, I thank
Ev - 'ry day I'll come to thank

You, oh, I thank You.
You, oh, to thank You.

25
I Could Sing of Your Love Forever

Capo 3 (D)

Words and Music by
MARTIN SMITH

I Lift My Eyes

Words and Music by
DAVID CROWDER

I Love Your Love

Words and Music by
PAUL OAKLEY

Capo 4 (C)

With energy

Sometimes when I feel Your love as I walk along the busy street, I whisper Your name under my breath. And sometimes when I feel Your touch in the quiet place of my room,

love   Your   love,_____   'cause I've found____   it   to be   true,—

____   and I live—

____   to love____ You,   too._____

Chords Used in This Song

G   D   C   Em   C/E

28 Intimacy

Words and Music by
MATT REDMAN

Tenderly, with awe

1. One thing my heart is set up-on, one
2. To look up-on Your beau-ty, Lord, Your
3. Lord, since the day I saw You first, my

thing that I would ask: to
glo - ry and Your heart; to
soul was sat - is - fied; and

know You, Lord, as close as one could
know You close and clos - er still each
yet, be - cause I see in part, I'm

hope to on this earth.
day up - on this earth.
search - ing more to find.

Chorus

In - ti - ma - cy,⸺ O Je - sus,

in - ti - ma - cy.⸺ My

trea - sure will be⸺ O Je - sus, Your

in - ti - ma - cy.⸺

— Chords Used in This Song —

E2(sus)   E2   E/A   B7sus

29

I've Found Jesus

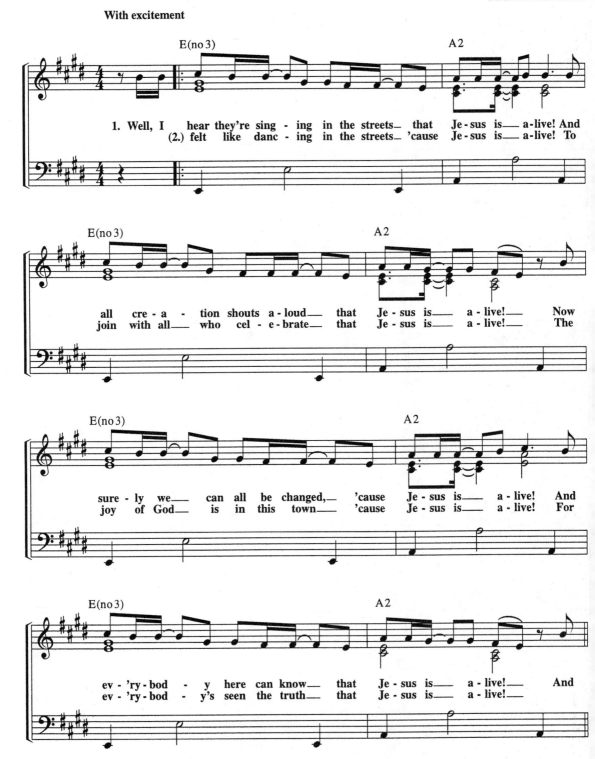

Words and Music by
MARTIN SMITH

With excitement

E(no 3)   A2

1. Well, I hear they're sing - ing in the streets— that Je - sus is— a-live! And
(2.) felt like danc - ing in the streets— 'cause Je - sus is— a-live! To

E(no 3)   A2

all cre - a - tion shouts a-loud— that Je - sus is— a - live!— Now
join with all— who cel - e - brate that Je - sus is— a - live!— The

E(no 3)   A2

sure - ly we— can all be changed,— 'cause Je - sus is— a - live! And
joy of God— is in this town— 'cause Je - sus is— a - live! For

E(no 3)   A2

ev - 'ry - bod - y here can know— that Je - sus is— a - live!— And
ev - 'ry - bod - y's seen the truth— that Je - sus is— a - live!—

Chords Used in This Song

30

I Want to Know You
(In the Secret)

Words and Music by
ANDY PARK

Capo 1 (G)

With energy

1. In the se - cret, in the qui - et place,
2. I am reach - ing for the high - est goal,

in the still - ness, You are there.
that I might re - ceive the prize.

In the se - cret, in the qui - et ho - ur I wait on - ly for You,
Press - ing on - ward, push - ing ev - 'ry hin - drance a - side, out of my way,

'cause I want to know You more.
'cause, I want to know You more.

Chords Used in This Song

31

I Will Exalt Your Name

Capo 2 (D)

Words and Music by
JEFFREY B. SCOTT

♦ CODA

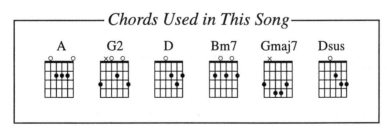

I Will Never Be the Same

Words and Music by
PAUL OAKLEY and KEVIN JAMIESON

Meditatively

I will nev-er be the same, now that I have seen the cross, and how You took up-on Your-self the full-ness of the wrath of God.

33

Jesus, We Love You

Words and Music by
**JOHN HARTLEY
and PHIL MADEIRA**

Jesus, Friend of Sinners

Words and Music by
PAUL OAKLEY

With energy

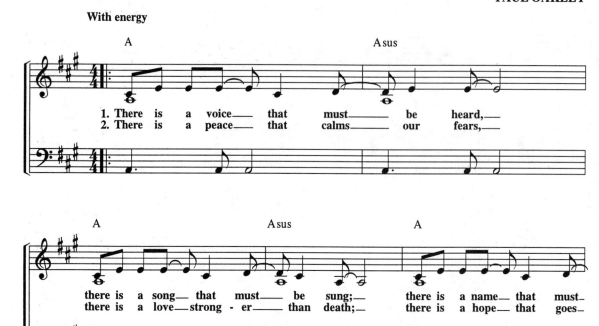

1. There is a voice___ that must___ be heard,___
2. There is a peace___ that calms___ our fears,___

there is a song___ that must___ be sung;___ there is a name___ that must___
there is a love___ strong-er___ than death;___ there is a hope___ that goes___

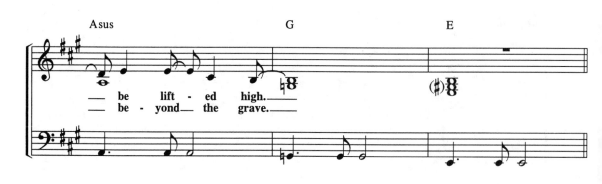

___ be lift - ed high.___
___ be - yond___ the grave.___

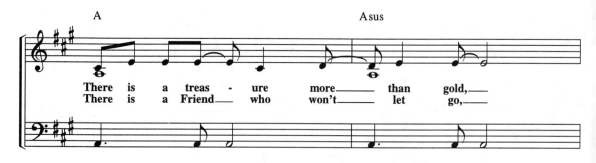

There is a treas - ure more___ than gold,___
There is a Friend___ who won't___ let go,___

Chords Used in This Song

Knowing You

35

Words and Music by
GRAHAM KENDRICK

Quietly

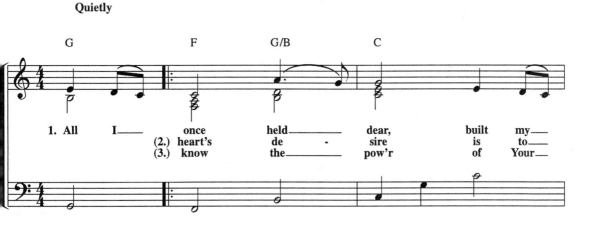

1. All I once held dear, built my
(2.) heart's de - sire is to
(3.) know the pow'r of Your

life up - on, all this world re -
know You more, all to be found in
ris - en life, and to know You

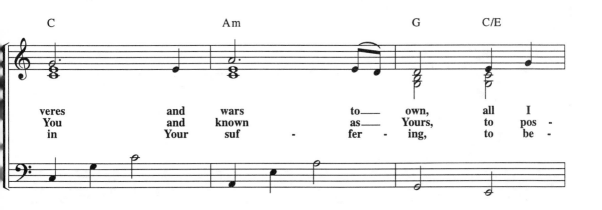

veres and wars to own, all I
You and known as Yours, to pos -
in Your suf - fer - ing, to be -

once thought gain I have— count - ed——
sess by faith what I— could—— not——
come like You in Your— death,—— My—

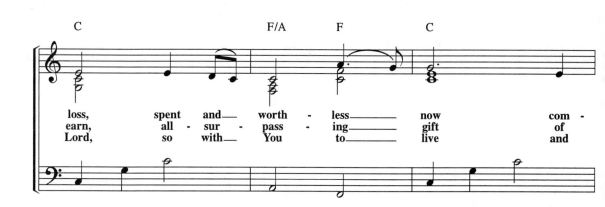

loss, spent and— worth - less—— now com -
earn, all - sur - pass - ing—— gift of
Lord, so with— You to—— live and

pared to— this. Know - ing
right - eous - ness.
nev - er— die.

You, Je - sus,—— know - ing You. There

36

Learning to Love You

Capo 2 (D)

Brightly

Words and Music by
PAUL OAKLEY

Keyboard (Guitar)

1. I'm learn-ing— to love— You,
(2.) — You,

to love and— to trust— You;
to love and— to trust— You.

I'm learn-ing— to give— You
And teach me— to give— You

all that— I am.
all that— I am.

Let Everything That Has Breath

Driving

Words and Music by
MATT REDMAN

Verse

1. Praise— You in the morn - ing,— praise— You in the eve - ning,—
2. Praise— You in the heav - ens,— join - ing with the an - gels,—

praise— You when I'm young and when I'm old.—
prais - ing You for - ev - er and a day.—

Praise— You when I'm laugh-ing,— praise— You when I'm griev-ing,—
Praise— You on the earth now,— join - ing with cre - a - tion,—

praise— You ev - 'ry sea - son of the soul.—
call - ing all the na - tions to Your praise.—

If

38

Let It Rain
(We Have Prayed That You Would Have Mercy)

Words and Music by
PAUL OAKLEY

Capo 2 (D)

Keyboard:
Guitar:

Lyrics:

We have prayed that You would have mercy; we believe from heaven You've heard. Heal our land, so dry and so thirsty; we have

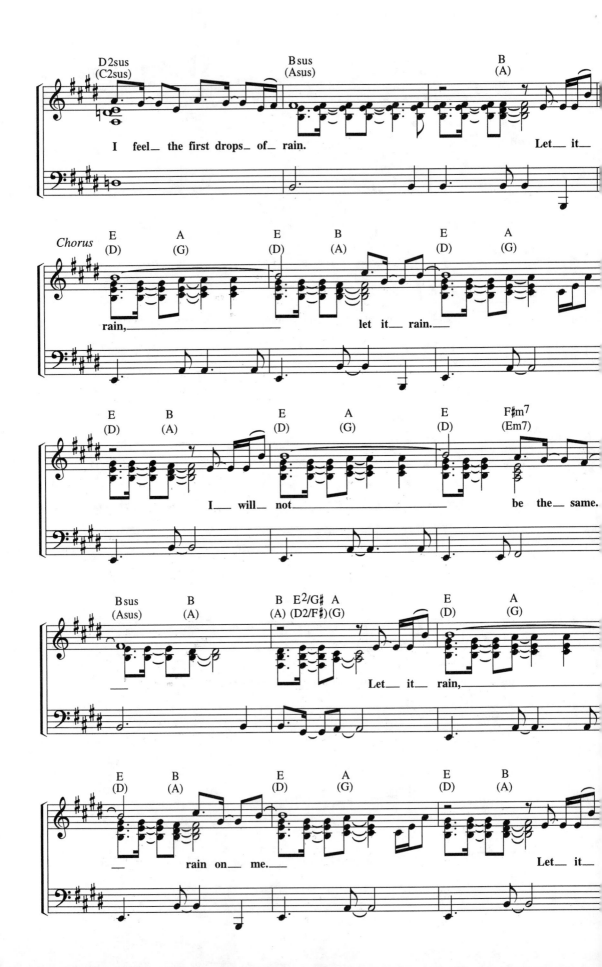

pour down___ on___ me,___ let it___ rain.___ Let___ it___ rain,

let___ it___ rain, let___ it___ rain, let___ it___ rain on___ me.

1.
B
(A)

2.
B
(A)

D.C. | Last time only

B
(A)

E
(D) *Fine*

We___ have___ let___ it___ rain on___ me.___

Chords Used in this Song

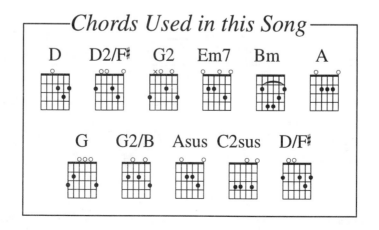

D   D2/F♯   G2   Em7   Bm   A

G   G2/B   Asus   C2sus   D/F♯

39

Let Your Glory Be Revealed

Words and Music by
TOM LANE

40

Let Your Glory Fall

Words and Music by
MATT REDMAN

1. Lord, let Your glory fall as on that ancient day; songs of enduring love, and then Your glory came.
2. Voices in unison, giving You thanks and praise, joined by the instruments, and then Your glory came.
3. A sacrifice was made, and then Your fire came; they knelt upon the ground, and with one voice they praised.

Lovely Noise

41

Words and Music by
GREG and **REBECCA SPARKS**

With a strong beat

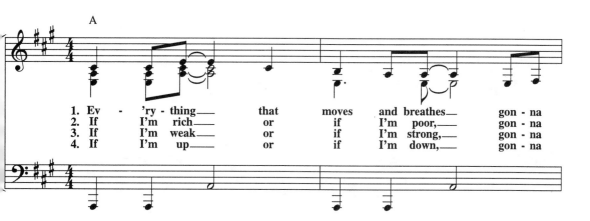

1. Ev - 'ry - thing___ that moves and breathes___ gon - na
2. If I'm rich___ or if I'm poor,___ gon - na
3. If I'm weak___ or if I'm strong,___ gon - na
4. If I'm up___ or if I'm down,___ gon - na

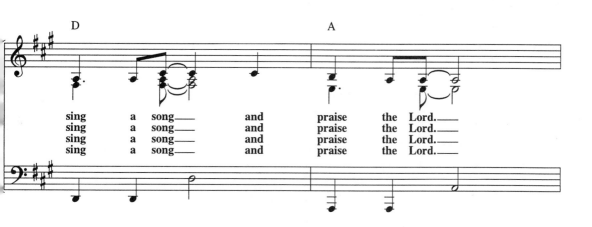

sing a song___ and praise the Lord.___
sing a song___ and praise the Lord.___
sing a song___ and praise the Lord.___
sing a song___ and praise the Lord.___

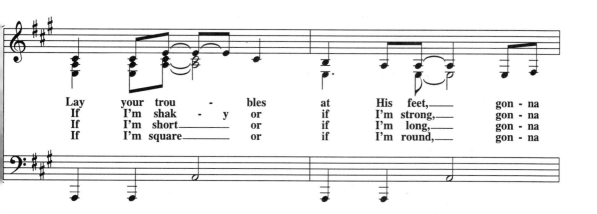

Lay your trou - bles at His feet,___ gon - na
If I'm shak - y or if I'm strong,___ gon - na
If I'm short___ or if I'm long,___ gon - na
If I'm square___ or if I'm round,___ gon - na

Make a Joyful Noise/ I Will Not Be Silent

Rhythmically

"Make a Joyful Noise" - Words and Music by Terry Butler

"I Will Not Be Silent" - Words and Music by David Crowder

43

My Dwelling Place

Words and Music by
JOHN HARTLEY

Now to Live the Life

Words and Music by
MATT REDMAN

1. Man - y are the words— we speak,— we pray— that
(2.) pre - cious are the words— we speak,—

man - y are the songs— we sing;—
pre - cious are the songs— we sing;—

man - y kinds of of - fer - ings,—— but now to live— the life.—
pre - cious all these of - fer - ings,—— but now to live— the life.—

1.   *(Repeat verse 1)*

One Thing Remains

Words and Music by
MATT REDMAN

Open the Doors of Praise

**Words and Music by
IAN WHITE**

O Sacred King

Words and Music by
MATT REDMAN

Worshipfully

O__ Sa-cred King, O__ Ho-ly King, how can I hon-or You right-ly,__ hon-or that's fit for Your name? O__ Sa-cred Friend, O__ Ho-ly

Pour Out Your Love

Words and Music by
CHERI KEAGGY

Prayerfully

I cher-ish these mo-ments with You, my Lord, when my

spir-it is will-ing to rest in Your pres-ence. True con-

tent-ment be-gins here with You, my Lord, as I

cher - ish——— these mo - ments——— with——— You.

Pour out——— Your love   to   me.——————   Let it———

fill   my——— heart——————   to   the   deep - est——— part.———

Pour out——— Your love   so that   You might——— see——————   a re - flec-

Pour Out Your Spirit

Words and Music by
TOM LANE

and ev - 'ry na - tion___ to the God of___ love___ and ho - li - ness. Let the fi - re of Your Spir - it___ burn.___

(vs. 2) **Pour out Your mercy, Lord, on Your people. (3 times)**
Let it reign. Let it reign.

(vs. 3) **Pour out Your fire, Lord, on Your people. (3 times)**
Let it reign. Let it reign.

Chords Used in this Song

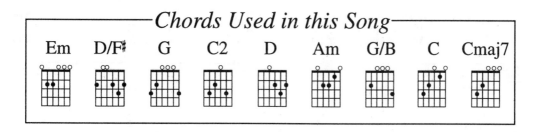

Em D/F# G C2 D Am G/B C Cmaj7

50 Pre-Revival Days

Words and Music by
IAN WHITE

1. We're reach-ing out to You a-gain.___ We're
(2.) look-ing at our lives a-gain.___ Your
4. Je-sus out in front a-gain.___

in the up-per room a-gain.___ We
love has filled our eyes a-gain.___ We
Je-sus on our tongues a-gain.___ We're

feel the Spir-it's wave, we're in___ pre-re-viv-al days.
cher-ish Your em-brace, we're in___ pre-re-viv-al days.
ris-ing up in faith to see___ re-viv-al days.

We're kneel-ing on the floor a-gain.___ We're
We're pray-ing for the lost a-gain.___ The
We're pray-ing for our land a-gain.___ You've

Reign on Me

51

Words and Music by
CHERI KEAGGY

With excitement

Reign on me, Lord, won't You reign on me. I'm giv-ing You all of me; Lord, won't you

3rd time to CODA

reign on me.

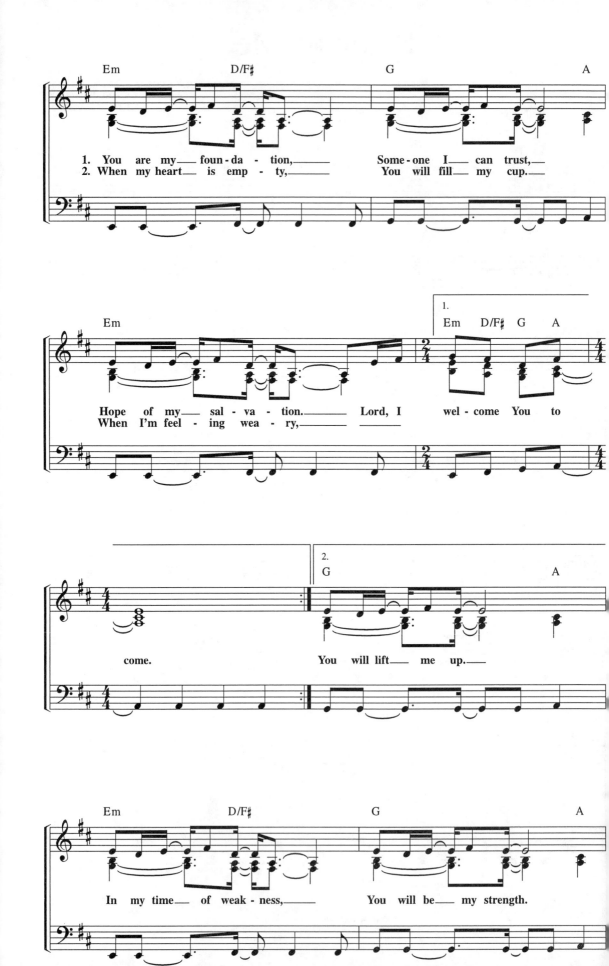

Touch me with Your pow - er; Lord, I wel - come You to

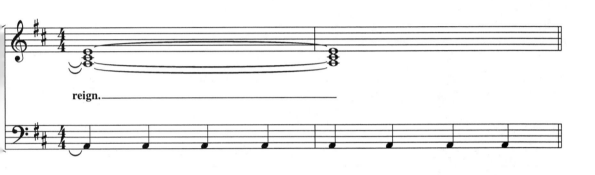

reign.

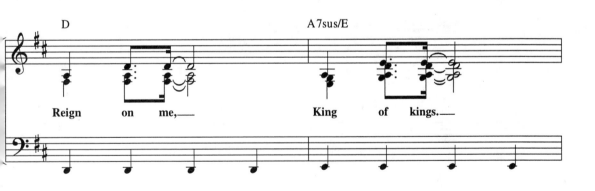

Reign on me, King of kings.

Lord, I'm giv - ing You ev - 'ry - thing.

52

Revival Sound

**Words and Music by
KEVIN JAMIESON, PAUL OAKLEY
and AMANDA WOLFRAM**

1. I hear a sound in the at - mos - phere,
2. I'm o - ver here, now I'm o - ver there.
3. It's like the sound of a mil - lion hors - es,
4. It's like the roar of the crowd on the ter - rac - es,

there's some - thing break - ing, some - thing's turn - ing 'round.
There's some - thing mov - ing, I can feel it now.
it's like a land - slide, rock fall tum - bling down.
it's like a trem - or quak - ing in the ground.

No more mess - ing a - round,

Can't beat_ it. It's the sound_ of heav - en com - ing down._

-ter fall - ing down._____ Re - viv - al sounds,_

_ re - viv - al sounds,_ re -

viv - al sounds._____ Re -

Chords Used in This Song

A G/A D Bm7 G A/D E A7 F#m/A

Sanctify

53

Words and Music by
MARTIN SMITH and STUART GARRARD

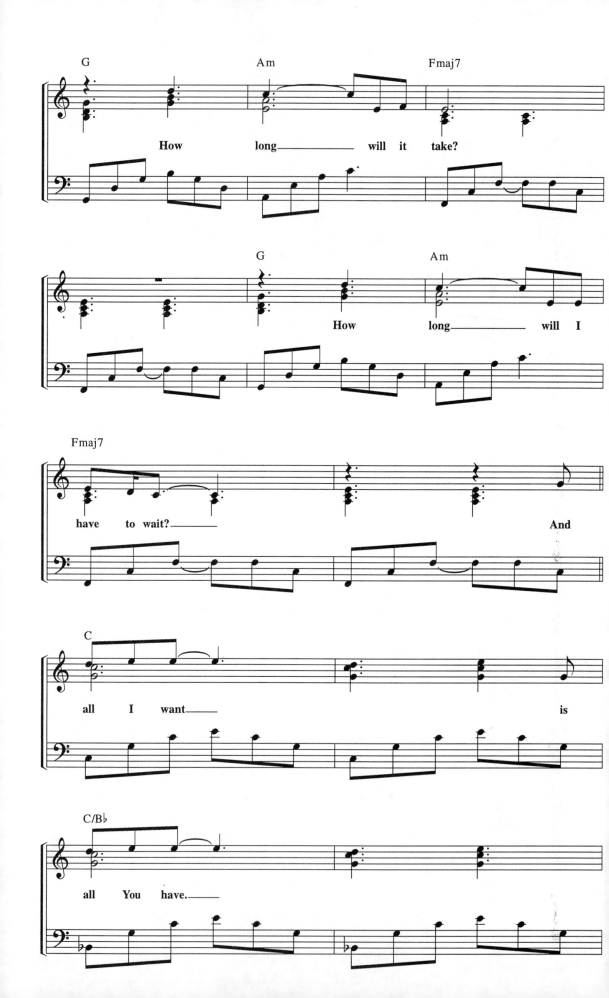

love.

Lift-ed up,_____ I've climbed with the strength I have

right to this moun-tain-top. Look-ing out,_____ the

cloud's get-ting big - ger now; it's time to get read - y now.

Chords Used in This Song

Am   C   Fmaj7   G   C/B♭   Fmaj7/A   C/G

Shake the Heavens

54

Words and Music by
DAVID RUIS

With conviction

1. Not to a moun-tain, not to a tem-ple
2. Not to a sys-tem, not just re-li-gion,

made of wood and stone,
emp-ty words and rules,

not to the an-gels, to the saints as-sem-bled,
but to true sal-va-tion, ho-ly me-di-a-tion,

to God on His right-eous throne;
sprin-kled blood of the One who rules;

not just a trem-bling of my flesh,

Chords Used in This Song

55 Sing Like the Saved

Words and Music by
MATT REDMAN

Joyfully

1. We're gon - na sing like the saved,_____
2. A joy - ful noise we will make,_____
3. You put Your joy in our hearts,_____
4. We're gon - na dance like the saved,_____

we're gon - na sing like the saved,_____
a joy - ful noise we will make,_____
You put Your joy in our hearts,_____
we're gon - na dance like the saved,_____

we're gon - na sing like the saved,_____
a joy - ful noise we will make,_____
You put Your joy in our hearts,_____
we're gon - na dance like the saved,_____

we're gon - na sing like the saved._____
a joy - ful noise we will make._____
You put Your joy in our hearts._____
we're gon - na dance like the saved._____

—— Chords Used in This Song ——

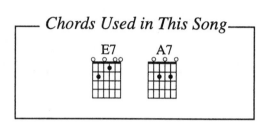

56

Sweet Mercies

Words and Music by
DAVID RUIS

Moderately

It's our con-fes-sion, Lord, that we are weak,

so ver-y weak, but You are strong.

And though we've noth-ing, Lord, to

lay at Your feet, we come to Your feet and say,

The Cross Has Said It All

57

Capo 2 (G)

Words and Music by
MATT REDMAN and MARTIN SMITH

1. The cross has said it all, the
(2.) cross has said it all, the

cross has said it all.
cross has said it all.

I can't de-ny what You
I nev-er rec-og-nized

have shown,
Your touch

the cross speaks of a God of love;
un-til I met You at the cross.

there dis-played for all to see,
We are fall-en, dust to dust;

Je-sus Christ, our on-
how could You do this

Chords Used in This Song

G   Am7   Bm7   C2   D   C   Em   F

58

The Eyes of My Heart

Words and Music by
MATT REDMAN

The Heart of Worship
(When the Music Fades)

Words and Music by
MATT REDMAN

59

1. When the mu-sic fades, all is stripped a-way,
2. King of end-less worth, no one could ex-press

— and I sim-ply come;
— how much You de-serve.

long-ing just to bring something that's of worth
Though I'm weak and poor, all I have is Yours,

— that will bless Your heart.
— ev-'ry sin-gle breath.

all a‑bout You,___ all a‑bout You,___ Je‑sus.

I'm sor‑ry, Lord, for the thing___ I've made___ it, when it's

all a‑bout You,___ all a‑bout You,___ Je‑sus.___

Chords Used in This Song

D2   A2   Em7   Asus   D/F♯   A2/C♯   G   A7sus

60

The Lamb Who Was Slain

Words and Music by
SAL OLIVERI and
JEFF NELSON

1. You have o-pened the door of the
(2. You came) down as a man, and You

rich-es of God, and poured out Your life for the
suf-fered the cross. The King of the heav-ens be-

lost; the Lamb who was slain. You e-
came the Lamb who was slain. But our

rased all our sin, pur-chased men with Your blood,
God raised You up, and our tongues now con-fess

The Mystery of God

Capo 1 (F)

Words and Music by
IAN WHITE

The Prayers of the Saints

Words and Music by
MATT REDMAN

With awe

1.2. Are the prayers of the saints— like
3.4. Are the songs of the saints— like

sweet smell - ing in - cense, are the prayers of the saints— like
sweet smell - ing in - cense, are the songs of the saints— like

sweet smell - ing in - cense to Your heart, to Your
sweet smell - ing in - cense to Your heart, to Your

1.3. | 2.4.
heart? | heart?
heart? | heart?

1. Let these
2.3. Let these

To Speak Your Name

63

Capo 3 (A)

Words and Music by
JAMI SMITH
and **JANET HUBBELL**

With much emotion

Chords Used in This Song

64

Undignified
(I Will Dance, I Will Sing)

Capo 2 (D)

Words and Music by
MATT REDMAN

Chords Used in This Song

65

We Fall Down

Words and Music by
CHRIS TOMLIN

Capo 2 (D)

66 What a Friend I've Found

Words and Music by
MARTIN SMITH

Slow and steady

1. What a Friend I've found, clos - er that a broth - er;
2. What a hope I've found, more faith - ful than a moth - er.

I have felt Your touch, more in - ti - mate than lov - ers.
It would break my heart to ev - er lose each oth - er.

Je - sus, Je - sus,

Je - sus, Friend for - ev - er.

Chords Used in This Song

C   Dm   F   C/E   Am   G/B   G/D

67

What I Have Vowed

Capo 1 (C)

Words and Music by
MATT REDMAN

1. Lord, I am not my own, no longer my own, living now for You, and ev'ry-thing I think, all I say and do is for You, my Lord.
2. Now tak-ing up the cross, walk-ing on Your paths, hold-ing out Your truth, run-ning in this race, bow-ing ev'ry day, all for You, my Lord.
3. Earth has noth-ing I de-sire that lives out-side of You, I'm con-sumed with You. Treas-ures have no hold, noth-ing else will do, on-ly You, my Lord.

And what I have vowed I

68

When I Needed a Savior

Words and Music by
MATT REDMAN

Slowly, with a gentle rhythm

1. Look-ing back on time, seek-ing to re-mind my-self of all Your mer-cies, I can tes-ti-fy on ev-'ry page of life, Your grace just keeps un-fold-ing
2. Ev-er since the day I looked up-on the cross I've re-al-ized Your mer-cy. For ev-'ry stage of life, sweet and bit-ter times, Your grace just keeps un-fold-ing

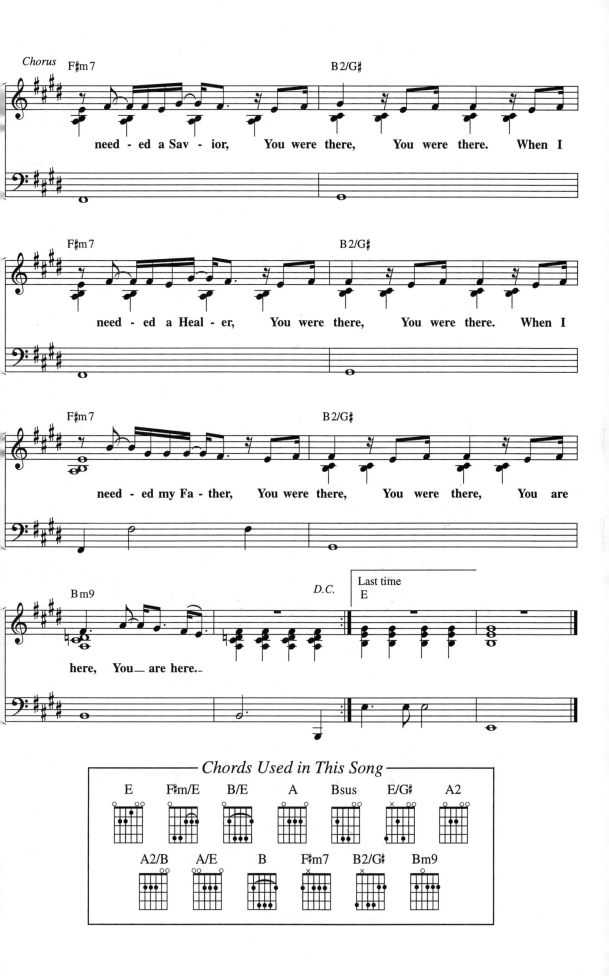

69 Worshipping the Living God

Words and Music by
IAN WHITE

You Alone

**Words and Music by
JACK PARKER and
DAVID CROWDER**

71 You Are Merciful to Me

Words and Music by
IAN WHITE

Prayerfully

You are mer-ci-ful— to me, You are mer-ci-ful— to me, You are

mer-ci-ful— to me, my Lord.— You are

Ev-'ry day— my dis-o-be-dience grieves Your lov-ing heart;— but

then re-deem-ing love breaks through, and caus-es me— to

You Are My King

Words and Music by
BILLY JAMES FOOTE

D.C. al Coda

⊕ CODA

Chords Used in This Song

You Are My Rock

Words and Music by
JOEL AUGE

Lord, let Your rain fall down, 'cause You are my rock, You are my rock.

Wash a-way the sand and the clay, 'cause You are my rock, You are my rock.

74

You Have Given Me New Life
(Over Me)

Words and Music by
NATHAN and DAVID FELLINGHAM

Song lyrics beneath the music:

and mer - cy, o - ver me in a
so free, o - ver me Your un -

flood of pow'r. end - ing love.

end - ing love.

vs. 2 **I've never had a friend like You;**
All that You've promised You will do.
I'm drinking from the fountain that will never run dry,
I'm living in the joy of a heart that's purified.
I'm walking now with You, and all I have is Yours;
Take my life.

Chords Used in this Song

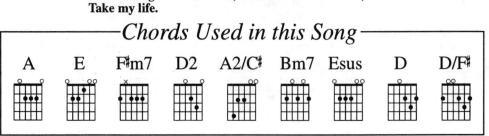

A   E   F#m7   D2   A2/C#   Bm7   Esus   D   D/F#

75

You Paid It All

Words and Music by
JOHN HARTLEY
and GARY SADLER

1.,3. There laid a price upon our heads, the cost of life required
(2.) stole the fear that plagued our race, You tore the shadow from

a death; our enemy demanded blood.
Your face; we run to You, no need to hide.

The sentence hanging
Such joy is rising

over us was nailed with You upon the cross; Your
from our hearts with songs of praises to our God, for

remedy was Your love. And You,
heaven's gates are open wide. For You,

76 You're Worthy of My Praise

Words and Music by
DAVID RUIS

Chords Used in This Song

(Appendix A)

Index of Songs by Key

Key of A

Key of A minor

Key of A flat

Key of B

Key of B minor

Key of C

Key of C minor

Key of D

Key of D flat

Key of E

Key of E minor

(Appendix B)

Index of Songs by Tempo

Up-tempo

Mid Up-tempo

Mid-tempo

Slow Mid-tempo

Slow

(Appendix C)

Index of Songs by Project

CyberSonic Song Source, Vol. 1

Encounter - Live At Usher Hall

Passion: Better Is One Day

Matt Redman: The Heart Of Worship

Revival Generation: I Could Sing of Your Love Forever

Revival Generation: Let Your Glory Fall

Revival Generation: Lovely Noise

Cheri Keaggy: There Is Joy In The Lord

Heaven & Earth